# THE ADVENTURES OF TOM SAWYER

## BY MARK TWAIN

# #1 A Song for Aunt Polly

Adapted by Catherine Nichols
Illustrated by Amy Bates

D1411085

ES
LE
KS
RK

Text copyright © 2004 by Barnes & Noble, Inc.
2004 Barnes & Noble Books

Adapted by Catherine Nichols
Illustrations copyright © 2004 by Amy Bates
Designed by Jennifer Markson

ISBN 0-7607-3963-3
Printed and bound in China

10 9 8 7 6 5 4 3 2 1

# Contents

## Time for a Lesson

Tom Sawyer had just eaten lunch.

It was a very big lunch,

but he was still hungry.

Tom was always hungry.

He tiptoed into the parlor,

looking for candy.

He found peppermints

in the candy dish.

Just as Tom took one . . .

*. . . dong! Dong!*
There went the
grandfather clock!
It was time for his
piano lesson,
but Tom wanted to go
swimming with his friends.

"Tom!" Aunt Polly called.

She was coming down the stairs.

Oh, no! She would be sure

to make Tom go

to his piano lesson!

He looked around.

Where could he hide?

Tom heard Aunt Polly's footsteps.
They were getting closer
and closer and closer!
Tom had to find
somewhere to hide.
The closet!
That was a good place.
He dashed inside.

## Where's Tom?

Aunt Polly looked
around the parlor.
She did not see Tom—
only the cat, on the sofa.
"Where can that boy be?"
she asked the cat.

Aunt Polly put on her glasses.

She still did not see Tom.

Aunt Polly knew Tom

didn't want to go to his lesson.

"Every week he tries to hide,"

she told the cat.

"I'll find that rascal.
He can't hide from me!"
Aunt Polly took a broom.
She poked it under the sofa.
No Tom.

Aunt Polly looked
everywhere for Tom.
She looked behind
the drapes.

She looked behind the grandfather clock.

She looked inside a large urn.

Still, there was no Tom.

"That boy isn't here,"
Aunt Polly said.

"Maybe he's in the garden."

In the closet,

Tom's nose twitched.

He tried to stop the sneeze,

but it came anyway.

*ACHOO!*

Aunt Polly threw open
the closet door.
She had found Tom!
Tom looked up.
He smiled at his aunt.
"Care for a peppermint,
Aunt Polly?" he asked.

## At the Swimming Hole

"Tom!" Aunt Polly cried.

"Why are you in the closet?"

Tom saw the piano book

in his aunt's hand.

He thought fast.

"I was looking for my

piano book," he said.

"It's time for my lesson."

"That's why I was calling you!"

Aunt Polly said.

"Didn't you hear me?"

"No, Ma'am," Tom said.

He kept his fingers crossed
behind his back.
"Well, hurry along,"
his aunt said,
"or you'll be late!"

Tom walked along.
He came to two paths.
One path led to
his piano lesson.
The other one led to
the swimming hole.
Tom wasn't sure
which path to take.

Then he felt the sun.

It was so very warm on his face!

He looked up at the sky.

It was so very blue!

Tom made up his mind.

It was too nice a day

for a piano lesson.

He was going swimming!

Tom met his friends
at the swimming hole.
*Splish! Splash!*
He jumped into the water.
He swam and played.
What a great time he had!
Tom wished he could stay longer,
but he knew Aunt Polly
was waiting for him.

Tom dried off.

He was careful to wipe up

every drop of water.

Tom thought this

was very clever.

Aunt Polly would not know

he had been swimming, now.

She would think he had been

at his piano lesson!

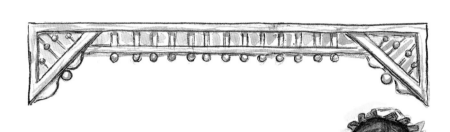

## A Song for
## Aunt Polly

Aunt Polly was waiting
for Tom on the porch.
Tom hummed as
he skipped up the steps.
"You sound happy,"
said Aunt Polly.
"Did you enjoy your lesson?"
"Yes, Aunt," said Tom.
He crossed his fingers
behind his back.

"It's such a nice day,"
Aunt Polly said.
"Many boys would have
liked to go swimming."
"That's true, Aunt," Tom said.
"Many boys," said Aunt Polly,
"but not you, right Tom?"

"No, Ma'am," Tom said.
He crossed his fingers
behind his back again.
Aunt Polly felt Tom's shirt.
Tom knew she wanted
to see if it was damp.
He was glad he had
dried off so carefully.

"Your shirt is dry!"

said Aunt Polly.

She smiled at Tom.

"You did not go swimming.

You went to your lesson."

She kissed Tom

on the top of his head.

"Tom!" Aunt Polly cried.

She felt his hair.

It was still wet.

Tom had dried his clothes,

but . . . *uh, oh!*

He had not dried his hair!

Tom looked up
at Aunt Polly.
She was frowning.
Tom felt sad.
He had upset his aunt.
"I'm sorry," Tom said.
"Don't be angry!"

*Uh, oh,* thought Tom.
She was *still* frowning.
How could he
make her happy?

Then Tom had an idea.

He went inside.

He sat at the piano.

He began to play

his aunt's favorite song.

He tried not to miss any keys.

Aunt Polly stopped frowning.

She hummed a little of the tune.

Then she started to sing.

Tom soon joined in.

Aunt Polly wasn't angry anymore.

That made Tom happy.

Playing the piano was fun!

Next week, he *would*

go to his lesson.

"I promise, Aunt!" Tom said.

Tom couldn't cross his fingers

when he was playing the piano . . .

so he crossed his toes,

just in case.